# The World's Best Salesman Jokes

# The World's Best Salesman Jokes

John Gurney

Illustrations by Rik Kemp

ANGUS
& ROBERTSON
PUBLISHERS

*ANGUS & ROBERTSON PUBLISHERS*

*Unit 4, Eden Park, 31 Waterloo Road,
North Ryde, NSW, Australia 2113, and
16 Golden Square, London W1R 4BN,
United Kingdom*

*First published in Australia
by Angus & Robertson Publishers in 1987
First published in the United Kingdom
by Angus & Robertson (UK) in 1987
Reprinted 1988*

*Copyright © John Gurney 1987*

*National Library of Australia
Cataloguing-in-publication data.*

*The World's best salesman jokes.*

*ISBN 0 207 15629 8.*

*1. English wit and humor. 2. Sales personnel
– Anecdotes, facetiae, satire, etc. I. Gurney, John,
1929– . II. Kemp, Rik.*

*828'.0208*

*Typeset in 12/13 pt Goudy
by Midland Typesetters
Printed in the United Kingdom by
Hazell Watson & Viney Ltd*

# INTRODUCTION

The stories that are told about company representatives together depict a way of life. The typical salesman is a man who lives well in first-class hotels, makes a packet by manipulating his swindle sheet, drinks enough to be an important guest at every pub in his territory, and has at least one woman constantly available in every town.

Having been on the road as a rep most of my life, I can assert that this is quite the opposite to a true picture (no-one will believe this, of course).

My guess is that most of these stories were made up by company reps themselves as a form of wish-fulfilment. They reflect the territory not as it is, but as the reps would like it to be. As Arthur Miller has it in the closing scene of *Death of a Salesman*: "A salesman is got to dream, boy. It comes with the territory."

We hope that there will be many a salesman stuck in a second-class country hotel who finds this book agreeable company in his lonely job, and that he gets some good laughs from the gags he hasn't already heard.

John Gurney

A salesman is a man with a smile on his face, a shine on his shoes, and a lousy territory.

A young man came to the underwear department of a men's store with a complaint. He was attended to by a young woman.

"I want to return these underpants please."

"Certainly, sir. What's wrong with them?"

"They're . . . not suitable."

"In what way, sir?"

"Well, I'll put it this way. Do you know St Paul's Cathedral?"

"Yes, of course."

"And do you know the ballroom underneath?"

"Wait a minute. There's no ballroom underneath."

"Right. And that's just what's wrong with these underpants."

Dave was in the city to buy a tractor and wanted to buy a present for Mabel. Very nervously he went into a lingerie shop. The salesgirl was very pleasant and helpful, and asked:

"How can I help you?"

"I want to buy one of those," Dave said, and blushed as he pointed to a bra on a dummy.

"Certainly, sir. What size?"

"Size? Oh gosh. I don't know."

"Well are they like coconuts?"

"Oh, no."

"Are they like grapefruit?"

"Oh, no."

"Oranges then?"

"No."

"Lemons?"

"Lemons? Ah, no."

"Well then, eggs?"

"Eggs. Yes. Eggs—poached."

A persistent salesman was told that his prospect was out, but he declined to leave. After nearly two hours the executive grew tired of being a prisoner in his own office, and let the salesman in.

"Angela told you I was out. How did you know I was here?"

"Easy. She was working."

A salesman in the Australian outback was driving from Cunnamulla to Dirranbandi in the late afternoon. He was being constantly troubled by kangaroos and emus running towards the headlights of his car. He stopped at a farmhouse and asked the farmer to put him up for the night.

"I suppose so. But there'd better be no hanky-panky with my beautiful nineteen-year-old daughter."

"Oh, gosh no. I'm a happily married man."

When they went inside the farmer's wife was cooking dinner. Their daughter was setting the table. She was indeed very beautiful. They turned in early, the farmer showing the salesman to his room.

During the night the farmer woke to hear a peculiar noise. He got out of bed and picked up the loaded shotgun standing beside the door. In the passage he could see a light under his daughter's bedroom door. He flung open the door just in time to catch the rep swinging one leg out of his daughter's bed. He up with the shotgun and let him have the left barrel—right through the stalk.

His victim let out an agonised scream and ran out of the house to his car. He drove the hundred kilometres to Dirranbandi with one hand, clinging to his injured member with the other. Around 3 am he knocked up the local GP who examined the affected part for a time in silence. Then he said:

"You have made a mess of it, haven't you? I'm afraid there's not much I can do for you, but I can put you onto a good man down in Brisbane."

"Is he a good specialist, doctor?"

"Well, he's not really a specialist. In fact he's not a doctor at all. He's a piccolo player, but he'll be able to show you which holes to put your fingers over when you want to take a leak."

Late one afternoon a rep drove up to the only hotel in a small town. He found the publican and asked:

"Can you give me a room for the night?"

"Like to, but I can't. Every room's taken."

"Blimey! You've got to fit me in somewhere. I've got to work the town tomorrow. Can you give me a bed in a room with somebody else?"

"Well, there is one bed vacant in a twin room, but I hesitate to put you in there because the fellow in the other bed snores so much. We've had complaints about him before."

"That's all right. I'll soon fix him. I'll take it."

Next morning after breakfast the rep came to the desk to settle his account. He was as bright as a button. The publican asked him:

"How did you sleep last night?"

"Extra good, thanks."

"You didn't have any trouble with your roommate's snoring?"

"Oh, no. I soon put a stop to that."

"What did you do?"

"Well, when I went into the room, he was already in bed. I just went over and gave him a kiss on the cheek and said, 'Goodnight darling,' and he sat up all night watching me."

A rep for McSporran & McHaggis was caught in torrential rain. It came down in sheets. He sent off a telegram to Glasgow:

"MAROONED BY FLOODS, WIRE INSTRUCTIONS."

Two hours later the reply came back:

"COMMENCE ANNUAL VACATION IMMEDIATELY."


S am was going to be on the road for several weeks so he had his mail forwarded to a client in the territory. When he arrived his client gave him a special delivery letter. He read it quickly and nearly passed out.

"What's the trouble?" asked his client. "You look ill."

"It's my wife. She's just had triplets, which we never expected. And take a look at this hospital bill."

"Congratulations! Now you know how it feels to be charged for more stock than you ordered."

The managing director of a department store came across a docket for more than $42 000, and immediately phoned down to the department manager:

"Have this assistant come up to my office at 9.30 tomorrow morning," he said.

Next morning Tom Trenery presented himself at the managing director's office.

"Ah! Trenery isn't it? My reason for sending for you this morning is that yesterday I came across a docket of yours in excess of $42 000. That is very commendable. It was very likely the biggest transaction ever made in the history of the store.

"What I want you to do is describe for me step by step how you made the sale. I can pass the information along to our sales trainers. Now, what was the first item the customer bought?"

"Three dozen trout-fishing hooks."

"I see. What happened then?"

"I sold him half a dozen reels of line, some sinkers, wet and dry flies, and a rod and reel. Next he needed heavy-duty clothing, a hat and a pair of thigh boots. I pointed out that rather than carry his gear backwards and forwards every weekend, he would be much better with a permanent base. I sold him one of our three-room prefabricated cabins. I mentioned that roads into the best spots were fairly rugged and persuaded him to buy a four-wheel-drive vehicle. Then there was the boat and the outboard motor. I think that was all, sir."

"You mean this customer just came in for fish hooks, and you sold him all that?"

"Well, no sir. He didn't come in for fish hooks at all."

"What did he come in for?"

"He just asked me for directions to maternity wear, so I said to him, 'You look like being in for rather a lame time, sir. Have you tried trout fishing?'"

A farmer caught a rep in bed with his wife and knocked him out cold. When the man came to he was in the barn. The farmer had screwed his dick into a vice as tight as he could and thrown the handle away. He was standing there sharpening up a big carving knife. The rep blurted:

"Crikey! You're not going to cut it off are you?"

The farmer handed him the knife.

"No son. You can do that. I'm just going to set fire to the barn."

A rep overnighting at a farmhouse was told:

"You can sleep out here on the sofa, but you'll be much more comfortable if you spend the night with Baby."

The rep had visions of great puddles in the middle of the bed, and replied:

"That's all right thanks. I'll sleep here on the sofa."

It wasn't very comfortable, and by morning he was stiff and sore. Next thing the door opened and in walked a lovely redhead about eighteen years old, wearing skimpy baby doll pyjamas that showed plenty of long shapely leg. She stopped when she saw the visitor.

"Who are you?" he asked.

"I'm Baby. Who are you?"

"Me? I'm the mug that spent the night on the sofa."

The proprietor of a long-established firm of wholesalers was interviewing an applicant for a position as sales representative. The candidate had the right experience, good references, was well spoken and turned out. He would have been ideal for the position except that he had a disconcerting mannerism. While he talked he kept winking. The employer decided to be frank with him.

"Look here. I'd like to give you this job. You're well dressed, well spoken, you've got good references and the sort of experience we're looking for. The only trouble is this trick you've got of winking all the time while you talk. I'm afraid it might put our customers off."

"No worries," the candidate replied. "All I've got to do to get rid of it is take a couple of aspirins. You watch. I've got some here somewhere."

So saying he began emptying his pockets onto the desk. The employer was startled to see dozens of packets of condoms piling up—multi-coloured ones, ribbed ones, heavy-duty varieties, and every known brand of standard condom.

"Here we are," said the rep. He swallowed two aspirins and his winking stopped at once. "Look at that."

"That's all very well. You've solved the problem of your winking, but look at all this stuff here. This is a very conservative business. We couldn't hire a man who was going to be womanising all over his territory."

"Oh, I wouldn't dream of it. I'm a happily married man."

"Then how do you account for all these things?"

"Simple. Did you ever go into a chemist, winking all the time, and ask for a packet of aspirins?"

A man went into a sporting goods shop.
"You know all that expensive fishing tackle you sold me when I was in here last time?"

"Yes sir."

"You know you told me it was well worth all the extra money because of all the fish I was going to catch with it?"

"Yes."

"Well, would you mind telling me again? I'm getting discouraged."

A footwear salesman, staying at a hotel, took a fancy to the housemaid. He offered her $25 for an hour in his room, but she replied that she wasn't a girl like that. She said that when she did it, it was just for love. Now he'd put her off and she couldn't get passionate if she wanted to. The salesman happened to mention that he was selling shoes and had an extremely good sample pair. The girl gave in, and took the salesman upstairs where she stripped completely and lay back on the bed.

The rep got going and was surprised and delighted to find the girl very responsive. First she wrapped her right arm around him, then her left leg, then her left arm and then her right leg. Of course her enthusiasm must have been due to his skill as a lover.

"I thought you said you couldn't get worked up," said the rep rather smugly.

"I'm not. I'm just trying on the shoes."

The general manager of a men's store called one of his salesmen up to his office at the end of the week.

"I'm sorry to have to tell you this, Yardley, but your figures are not good at all. In fact they are well below that of any other assistant in your section. Unless you pull your socks up, and get your figures up with the others', we'll have to let you go."

"I'm sorry, sir. Can you give me any advice on how to go about it?"

"Well, there is one idea you might like to try. It will probably sound silly, but it has been known to work for other salespeople. Get hold of a dictionary and go through it page by page, just glancing at every word. Once in a while you will come across a word that seems to you to be particularly powerful. Memorise it, and find ways of working it into your sales story."

The following week the GM sent for Yardley again.

"Well my boy, I don't know how you've done it but this week your figures have been greater than any other three people in your section. Congratulations."

"Thank you, sir. All I did was follow your advice. I got the dictionary out after tea on Friday night and spent nearly all weekend searching for those power words you told me about, and on Sunday afternoon I found one."

"Good. What was it?"

"Fantastic."

"Fantastic. Yes. That's a good word. Tell me how you used it in your sales story."

"Well, on Monday morning my first customer was a woman with a young boy. She told me he was a pupil at an expensive private school. I said, 'Fantastic!'

" 'Yes,' she said, 'He's a good student—always up near the top of his class.' I said, 'Fantastic!' She said, 'Yes and not only that, but he's good on the playing field as well. He's one of the best batsmen in his age group, he's won a medal for athletics, and he's represented his school in the inter-school swimming carnival.' I said, 'Fantastic!' She bought a jumper, two pairs of shorts, four pairs of long socks, and four sets of underclothes.

"My next customer was an elderly gentleman who told me he belonged to Glen Iris Bowling Club. I said, 'Fantastic!' He said, 'Yes. We played Sandringham last week and beat them by three ends.' I said, 'Fantastic!' He said, 'Yes, and the week before we beat Glen Waverley by four ends.' I said, 'Fantastic!' Well, he bought two pairs of bowling creams, three cream Viyella shirts, a cream jumper, four pairs of cream socks, and a pair of bowling shoes.

"And it's been like that all week. The more the customers boast about themselves, the more I go on saying, 'Fantastic!' and they buy and buy."

"That's very interesting. Just as a matter of interest, what did you say to the customers when they were boasting about themselves before you discovered this word, 'fantastic'?"

"Oh, I just used to say, 'Ah, bullshit!' "

A rep asked a farmer if he could spend the night, and the farmer replied:

"Sure. You can share a room with the little red-headed schoolteacher."

"Thanks. You needn't worry. I'm always a perfect gentleman."

"That's good," said the farmer. "So's the little red-headed schoolteacher."


A fter a number of years on the road, Sammy started his own import/export business. His little enterprise was coming along nicely. Some important principals were coming from Japan and he was most anxious to make a good impression. He hired a luxury car, picked them up at the airport, and drove them to a first-class hotel.

"You make yourselves comfortable here, and I'll be back at seven so we can have some dinner."

His visitors were suitably impressed. Right on seven Sammy was back to take them into the dining room. Their discussion proceeded nicely. As they were talking, Sammy noticed out of the corner of his eye Sir Gordon Squire, the internationally famous retailing magnate, sitting at a corner table. He at once had a brilliant idea for making a really big impression on the Japanese.

"Forgive me if I appear rude, gentlemen, but I've just seen Gordon Squire at a table across the room. He and I have some unfinished business. I wonder if you'd mind very much if I excused myself for a short while. It won't take very long."

The Japanese agreed at once and watched Sammy thread his way between the tables. They were very impressed that someone so young should be on speaking terms with Sir Gordon Squire. When he approached Sir Gordon's table, Sammy was most deferential.

"Pardon the intrusion, Sir Gordon. I have followed your career with great interest, starting as you did in a small way with one country store, and building up an empire of department stores and shopping centres that stretches right across the country. It is surely one of the nation's great success stories. Now I am starting off to build up an import/export business and I've come to ask you a small favour. At my table I have with me some important clients from Japan, and I'm very anxious to make a good impression on them. Do you think it might be possible, when you're leaving, to stop by my table and say, 'So long, Sammy. I'll give you a ring next week'?"

Sir Gordon had a quiet smile and said:

"Oh yes. I think we might arrange that."

He turned to his secretary.

"You remind me when we're leaving to stop at Sammy's table on the way out."

Sammy thanked him and returned to his clients, who were very impressed by all this. They returned to their discussion. Nearly an hour went by, and Sir Gordon and his secretary got up to leave. On his way out he stopped at Sammy's table and dropped his hand on Sammy's shoulder.

"So long, Sammy," he said. "I'll give you a ring next week."

Sammy looked up in annoyance.

"Piss off will you, Gordon? Can't you see I'm busy?"

Just after World War II, when many servicemen were being demobilised, a number of businesses had a policy that ex-servicemen were to receive preference in all job hiring situations. A group of women, who were former employees of a department store, felt that their livelihood was threatened. They set out to prove that the men could not do their jobs as well as women could. Their attempts were unsuccessful, even when one of their group had a male shop assistant fit her with a girdle. The leader of the group felt that it was time for her to take action herself. She went to the haberdashery counter. There was a man serving. She fixed him with a steely eye.

"I want some one inch elastic please."

"Certainly, madam. What length?"

"About from your navel to your knackers."

"Certainly, madam."

He began measuring off dozens of yards of elastic. The woman stopped him.

"Young man. Do you know where your knackers are?"

"Sure do, lady. Shaggy Ridge."

A salesman was spending the night with an old farmer and his attractive young wife. The farmer told him: "There's only one big old double bed, so you'll have to sleep with us. It'll be all right though. I'll sleep in the middle."

At the evening meal the salesman discovered that the farmer's wife was not only very attractive, but also an excellent cook. To top off a splendid meal she brought out a tray of freshly baked scones. The rep tried one and it was delicious. He was reaching forward for another when the farmer held his arm.

"Not now, son," he said. "Let's save them till the morning."

After a quiet evening around the radio the three headed for bed. The two men changed in the bathroom, while the young wife got ready in the bedroom. She was already in bed when the men came in. The farmer slept in the middle. The salesman soon got comfortable and after a time the trio went off to sleep.

In the early hours they were all woken up by a loud commotion in the yard behind the house. The farmer bounded out of bed.

"That damned fox," he exclaimed. "He's after my chickens again."

Seizing a loaded shotgun, he disappeared through the door into the night. His young wife rolled over and shook the salesman's arm.

"Are you awake?" she asked.

"Yes."

"He'll be gone for ages. Now's your chance. Slip out to the kitchen and get yourself a couple more scones."

A rep was involved in a nasty accident and had his penis cut off. As soon as he was well enough he went to his doctor to see if he could get some kind of replacement.

"Don't have any spares available at the moment, otherwise I could do a transplant for you."

"But doctor, you must have something."

"The only thing I've got that might do is a baby elephant's trunk."

"I'll take it. I've got to have something. Put it on."

The operation was successfully performed and several weeks later the rep took his wife to a garden party at the vicarage. They did not stay the whole afternoon, but at her insistence, left very early. As soon as they were out of earshot of the other guests she started:

"I was never so uncomfortable as when that thing kept coming up from under the table and taking the buns off the plate."

"You were uncomfortable? You don't know what it was doing with them!"

One of the greatest salesmen was the man who sold a farmer two milking machines when he only had one cow, and then accepted the cow as a down payment.

Two salesmen travelling together sought a night's accommodation at a farm. The farmer was an attractive widow who made them most welcome, and gave them an excellent dinner. When it was time for bed she said:

"You're both decent, respectable-looking men. Why don't you toss up? The loser sleeps in the spare room; the winner comes in with me."

Jack won the toss and had a really marvellous night.

After breakfast next morning they set off again. They drove several kilometres in silence and then Bill asked:

"How'd it go?"

"Really great. But this morning she got a bit worried and wanted my name and address. Well, you know what my wife's like. I gave her yours."

There was a bitter argument about this, and their friendship broke up completely. Then, about nine months later, Bill looked Jack up.

"You remember that widow? Well, I've just had a solicitor's letter . . ."

"I'm sorry I let you down, Bill, but what could I do?"

"As I was saying, I've had a solicitor's letter. The dear lady's passed away and left me the farm."

A salesman had the bad luck to get a flat tyre on a fairly steep hill right outside the grounds of a mental hospital. He unscrewed the nuts on the wheel and jacked up the side of the car. As he did so he became aware that one of the patients was leaning on the fence watching him with great interest.

He took off the wheel and replaced it with the spare, only to discover that the five nuts had rolled down the steep gutter, and fallen into a drain. There was no way that he could get them out. While he was grappling with this problem a voice behind him said:

"Why don't you just take one nut off each of the other three wheels, and use those?"

The salesman was impressed and said:

"That's pretty smart. How come you're in there?"

"I may be mad, but I'm not bloody stupid."


Two salesmen were having coffee together and one was telling the other:

"We've got a terrific sales competition going at our place. The fellow who writes the biggest percentage over target for the quarter gets a holiday for two in the south of France with all expenses paid. The fellow who's second highest gets a tailor-made suit with an extra pair of trousers, and the fellow who's third gets a dozen shirts."

The other rep looked gloomily at his coffee for a moment.

"We're having a sales competition at our place too. The fellow that wins it keeps his job."

A newsagent in a little shop near a railway station was really cross when a stationery salesman called. He said that one customer after another came to him to buy cigarettes, and nearly always the conversation would go like this:

"A packet of cigarettes, please."

"What brand?"

"Oh, Hallmark of course."

"Large or small?"

"Oh, large of course."

"Plain or filter?"

"Oh, filter of course."

Only then could he sell the customer his cigarettes.

"Why can't they just ask for a large packet of Hallmark filters? What am I supposed to be? A mind reader?"

"Yeah. How are you off for exercise books?"

"Do with a couple of packets."

"Feint ruled or special ruling?"

"Oh, feint ruled of course."

"Stapled or quarter bound?"

"Oh, stapled of course."

"48s, 64s, 80s, or 120s?"

"Oh, 64s of course."

Railway staff are always extremely helpful. When the train came into Blackall from Jericho, a rep was told to get a taxi to Tattersalls Hotel, as the town was some distance from the station. While he waited for a taxi he asked a porter:

"Why didn't they build the station nearer the town?"

The porter looked at him pityingly.

"I suppose they wanted it to be close to the train line."

The following night in Barcaldine the same rep was waiting for the Midnight Horror to get to Longreach. It was supposed to leave at 10.30. It was now 11.15 and there was no sign of it. He asked the stationmaster:

"How long will the train be?"

There was a quick calculation.

"Nine carriages."

It was in Milwaukee that the reps found out the answer to the question: what happens to a bartender who locks himself in his cold store?

It happened to the publican of a Milwaukee hotel one Saturday afternoon. He tried calling out and banging on the door, but the noise of the crowd and the radio broadcasting the races drowned him out. He was just beginning to accept the idea that he might be frozen solid when he had an inspiration that got him out in less than a minute.

What did he do?

He just turned the beer off.

A rep staying at a remote hotel was horrified when he visited the only toilet—a smelly earth closet down the backyard, surrounded by a cloud of hundreds of flies. He remonstrated with the publican:

"Look here. You've got to do something about that toilet down the back. I can't use it. There are flies everywhere."

"Don't worry about it," he was told. "Just wait two or three minutes and I'll be ringing the dinner bell."

"What good will that do?"

"They'll all come up to the dining room."


One rep who was a real identity was Percy. He worked for a rubber company selling tyres in Arizona. It wasn't the greatest territory in the States by any stretch, but Percy had been going round the dealers for so many years that he kept writing top figures for his company year after year.

One time his company's marketing director made a special trip out to see Percy. He commented on the excellent figures Percy continued to write year after year. Percy was philosophical.

"I may not be the greatest tyre salesman in Arizona," he said, "but I'd sure as hell hate to be out here selling tyres against me."

Years ago, in a country town, there were two chemists on opposite sides of the main street. This was back in the days when a chemist's display window was always divided up into dozens of small pigeonholes, and the chemist did his best to display one of everything.

A representative came to town travelling in Force baby food. He had relatively modern training in merchandising, and persuaded one of the chemists to completely empty his window and let him build a display of nothing else but Force baby food.

He worked over the weekend and the locals were amazed to see the transformation of the chemist's window. Crowds gathered round to watch. They had never seen anything like it. For days the shop always had a small crowd around it.

By the end of the week, the chemist on the other side of the street was fed up. He decided to make a change in his window. He put a small jar right in the centre space, and typed a small card to go with it that soon had the whole town laughing:

WHY USE FORCE WHEN VASELINE IS ONLY 1s 3d A JAR?

In Australia, in the days before company cars became the accepted thing, Bill was a north Queensland representative. He worked the whole of the north and the west from Rockhampton by public transport on a tour of duty that took twelve weeks to complete.

On one trip to Mount Isa and Cloncurry in the far north-west, he finished working the Isa late on a hot summer afternoon. At 5.30 it was still oppressively hot. The only transport to Cloncurry was a slow goods train with no passenger accommodation. Bill and one other rep carried their cases into the guard's van, and prepared themselves for a hot, dreary journey with the guard.

In those days there was no direct rail link between Mount Isa and Cloncurry. The line took a deep loop to the south through a tiny railway town called Duchess, which was about halfway. The train finally got under way. The night was still hot. Progress was slow and there were continual stops along the way. The reps would ask:

"What are we stopping for this time?"

The answers:

"We're taking on water."

"There's a cow on the line."

Bill had a good look at one of these cows, and when the train stopped again twenty minutes later because of a cow on the line, he studied it carefully and was prepared to swear it was the same cow. At last, after what seemed like hours of this, the train stopped again.

"What are we stopping for this time?"

"We're at Duchess. Do you feel like a beer?"

"Where's the pub?"

The guard pointed at a naked bulb about fifty metres across the tracks.

"No fear," said Bill. "I'm not going over there. The train might go without me."

"Well it can't go without me," said the guard, "and I'm going over."

The two reps and the guard were joined by the driver and the four picked their way across the tracks in the darkness to the pub. The light they were following lit up a big sign that said, "Cold Beer".

Bill's mouth began to water.

Inside, the cold beer turned out to be a wooden cask up on the counter, with a wet sack thrown over it. There was one other customer, a real western droving type, with the highheel boots and the broad-brimmed hat. Bill spoke to him:

"Will you have a drink with us?"

"Thanks, mate."

The beers were served and they all took a long pull. Bill asked the drover:

"You live round these parts?"

"No," came the reply. "I'm from the Centre. I'm down here on holidays. Boy, it's good to be back east again."

Goldy was in the knitwear business. He had a tidy little factory in New York, and turned out a product that was up near the top of the range. Sales were good locally, but he had excess capacity and decided to take up the slack by getting some orders out of the West Coast. He sent his rep Maurie down for two weeks to see what he could sign up. Maurie was only gone five days when Goldy got a phone call from the accountant at the San Francisco Hilton.

"We've had one of your men staying with us—Maurice Leberman—since last Monday. We're a little concerned at the amount of his account and would like you to confirm that it's okay."

"How much is involved?"

"Well, so far the total for accommodation, meals, liquor and special services is $4,792."

"But that's not possible."

"I've got the chits."

"You've got the chits! What do you think I've got?"

Late one night a salesman had a punctured tyre in the middle of nowhere, but he had no jack to change the wheel. The only thing was to walk to the farmhouse he had passed about two kilometres back to see if he could borrow one. As he walked, he rehearsed in his mind all the things the farmer might say to him:

"What's the idea of knocking me up at this hour of night?"

"Why should I lend my jack to you? I've never seen you before in my life."

"What sort of a driver are you that you don't carry your own jack anyway?"

"If I lend you my jack, how do I know I'll get it back?"

By the time he reached the farmhouse he was in a fine state. He hammered on the door. The farmer answered it:

"Yes, son. What's the trouble?"

"Never mind. You can keep your bloody jack."


Sandy the rep was a hard case. Faced with an operation he chose to go to a big Catholic hospital because it was the cheapest. Before he went into surgery he was visited by a religious sister who asked him questions like his name, address, place of work, age and so on. When she came to next-of-kin he was not very helpful.

"You mean there's no one at all we can put down as your closest relative?"

"Well, there's my sister. But she'd be no good. She's only a nun."

His visitor's hackles started to rise.

"What do you mean 'only a nun'? I'll have you know that she is married to the Son of God."

"Well, in that case, send the bill to my brother-in-law."

Three salesmen were lined up at the reception desk of a hotel when one of them had an idea. He said to the other two:

"Listen. Instead of getting three single rooms, why don't we just get the one room with three beds and share? Then we can save a few quid on our accommodation. The publican'll give us separate receipts for the full amount, won't you?"

The publican nodded a bit doubtfully. The other two reps fell in with the idea, and they were soon given the key to room seven on the first floor.

After they had gone upstairs, the publican thought this over, and then called his son.

"Listen. I've just booked three fellows into room seven upstairs. They reckon they're representatives, but I've got a horrible feeling they might be poofters and I don't want any of them round the place. Slip upstairs and have a look around. See what you can find out."

The son wasn't upstairs more than three minutes when he came back and reassured his father:

"It's okay Dad. They're reps all right."

"How can you be so sure? You were only up there a couple of minutes."

"Well Dad, I had a look through the keyhole, see? The first bloke had his foot up on the bed cleaning his shoe with the bedspread. The second bloke was having a piss in the wash basin. And the third bloke was looking out the window down the main street saying, 'Where the hell's a man going to get laid in a one-horse town like this?' They're reps all right."

A salesman came to a road junction with no signs whatever.

He asked a local who was walking by:

"Which is the road to Summerville?"

The man pointed off to the right.

"Is it far?"

"No, but when you get there you might wish it was a lot further."

A rep was stuck in a small town for more than two weeks and couldn't take it any longer. He went to the local brothel and said to the madam:

"Here's a hundred bucks. I want the worst blow job in the place."

"But for a hundred dollars you don't have to take the worst blow job. You can have the best."

"You don't understand. I'm not horny; I'm homesick."

A dealer called at a dairy farm and told the farmer that he was interested in buying a cow. The cows were all in the barn, and the farmer took him over to look at them. The dealer picked out an animal and, after some bargaining, paid the farmer $85.

But when they were putting the cow into the dealer's truck, the dealer discovered that the beast was blind. He turned on the farmer:

"You old fool. This cow's blind. How do you expect me to sell a cow that's blind?"

"Well, I just did."

A rep came to a river crossing that looked trea-
cherous so he asked a farmer if it was safe to take
his car through.

"Should be," said the farmer. "Reckon you'll get through
all right."

The rep started his car and drove into the water. After
a short distance he found himself in so deep that the water
was running into his windows. Extracting himself from
his car, he went back to the farmer and angrily demanded
to know why he had said the crossing was safe when the
water was so deep.

"Can't understand it at all," said the farmer. "The water
only came halfway up our ducks."


A salesman vacated his hotel room in a hurry one
morning, and left his briefcase behind. He soon
discovered his mistake and went straight back to the hotel
to pick it up. When he got there, however, he found that
the room was already occupied by a honeymoon couple.
Their voices carried out to the passage through the
transom.

"You see these, darling? No man has ever looked at
them before. And now they're yours. All yours."

There was a prolonged scuffling noise.

"You see this, darling? I've been saving it up all these
years, and now it's yours. All yours."

There was more scuffling. The rep lost patience and
called out:

"When you get to the black leather briefcase, it's mine.
All mine."

The sales manager was doing so well that he decided to upgrade the car that he was driving. He visited a prestige used car dealer, and expressed interest in a current model Mercedes, formerly owned by a very rich stockmarket speculator. The price was right, but he was puzzled by the mileage. The speedo showed only 4217 miles.

"Is that a genuine mileage?"

"Certainly is."

"You mean this fellow traded his car after it had only done 4217 miles?"

"That's right."

"What was wrong with it?"

"The ashtrays were full."


A rep was flying to a sales conference. It was his first experience in an aircraft, so he was a little nervous, but he tried not to let it show. He was very taken with the air hostess, and particularly flattered when she invited him to sit down the back with her. He asked her:

"Do many passengers get airsick?"

"Not many," she replied. "We usually spot them in advance and give them some sweets to suck."

"What if that doesn't work?"

"Oh, maybe we put a blanket over them, or even give them some oxygen."

"What if it still doesn't work?"

"Oh, then I bring them down the back to sit with me."

A salesman driving along a country road was amazed and delighted to see a really attractive, well-dressed woman hitchhiking on the side of the road. He stopped the car. As she started to get in he said:

"Look, miss. I think it's only fair to warn you that I'm a shocking driver. I'm always having accidents. But if you're prepared to take the risk, you're very welcome to the ride."

The young woman was quite unruffled, and buckled herself into the seat.

"That's okay," she said as he moved off. "But it's only fair to warn you that I'm a witch."

He just laughed. "Oh, yes."

"No, I mean it. I really am. I have supernatural powers. I could put you under my spell and make you turn into anything."

He just laughed all the louder. Then she put her hand on his knee and he turned into a motel.

Two religious sisters were driving together through the country at the end of the school vacation. Their car slowed to a halt, and they realised that they were out of petrol. They decided that one would stay with the car, while the other walked to the nearest station property to buy some petrol. When she got there, the owner had plenty of petrol, and was quite happy to give her a few litres, but he had nothing to put it in. Then she spied an old chamber pot lying in a corner. She asked:

"How about that?"

The unlikely vessel was cleaned up and filled, and the sister made her way back to the car, carrying the chamber pot in both hands. They took off the cap of the petrol tank, and were pouring the petrol in very carefully without a funnel, when a passing salesman stopped and gaped at them in amazement.

"Sister, I've heard about turning water into wine, but this is ridiculous."

He was a really hot sports car salesman, and he came to a farm where the whole yard was full of cars. Not derelicts. New cars. He could hardly believe it. Surely here was a man who couldn't resist a good story and a good product.

The farmer proved to be a very old man, while his wife was young and lovely. The old man was just not interested in buying another car. But he said to the salesman:

"I'm a sporting man. I'll make a bet with you. If you win I'll buy two of your cars. But if you lose, you give me that fancy sports car for nothing. Now I'll bet you I can do three things, and that you can't repeat all three of them."

The salesman thought about this. He loved a bet himself. Besides, he couldn't imagine this decrepit old wreck being able to do anything he couldn't do.

"You're on."

The farmer put his arms round his wife and gave her a long lingering kiss. Then he turned to the salesman and said:

"That's the first thing."

This was too good to be true. The salesman took the farmer's wife in his arms and gave her a kiss that Hollywood would have been proud of.

Next the farmer slipped his hand inside his wife's blouse until he cupped her breast. He stroked it and caressed it and fondled it.

"I must be dreaming all this," thought the salesman as he repeated the farmer's actions, and loved every minute of it.

Finally the old man pulled out his penis and wrapped it three times round a pencil.

The new salesman was back from his first country trip, and presented his "swindle sheet" to the sales manager, who went through it carefully.

"Let's see now. Petrol—that's okay. Accommodation—that's okay. Postage—yes. Entertainment—that could have been higher. Stationery—yes. What's this? One pair of handmade Italian shoes—$125. Is this some kind of joke?"

"No. I wore out a pair of shoes walking round my territory, and I bought a new pair."

"Did you. Well, you don't put them on your expense account. You buy your own Italian shoes. That's what we pay you a good salary for."

He crossed out the offending item, and reduced the total accordingly. Then he initialled the document and handed it back to the salesman.

"There. Give that to the accountant."

Two weeks later, after another country tour, the salesman again presented his "swindle sheet" to the sales manager, who again went through it carefully.

"Petrol—yes. Accommodation—yes. Meals—yes. Entertainment—yes. Stationery—yes. Postage—yes. That's okay. I'm glad to see there are no Italian shoes here this time."

He signed the paper and handed it to the salesman, who said:

"Oh, they're there. But just you find them."

The marketing manager was in the branch office stirring things up. One hot afternoon he came upon Dick Prendergast writing up his orders in the reps' room with no tie on.

"Here. You can't go round dressed like that. You're a representative of the company. Put a necktie on."

"Go and get fucked."

The marketing manager went to the branch manager and reported the exchange.

"This Prendergast. What can you tell me about him?"

"He's our best rep. His figures each year are more than any other two men we've got."

"Perhaps so. But you go and tell him not to address me in that fashion, and also to put on a necktie."

The branch manager conveyed this message to Prendergast, who merely replied:

"Go and have a shit."

He went back to the marketing manager.

"Did you tell him what I told you to?"

"Yes I did."

"What did he say?"

"He told me to go and have a shit."

"Did he? And what are you going to do now?"

"I'm going to have a shit. You can make your own arrangements."

One morning a rep was talking with a chemist who had let him put a large display of Snugg tampons in his showroom. The chemist interrupted their talk to attend to a young boy of about nine or ten.

"Yes, my boy. How can I help you?"

"I want a packet of tampons please."

The chemist took his money and began wrapping the purchase.

"Are these for your mother or your sister?"

"Neither. They're for me."

"Are they? What are you going to do with them?"

"I don't know for sure, but I saw on television that when you wear Snugg tampons you can go surfing, skin diving, hang gliding and horseback riding. I've never done any of those things, but now I'll be able to."

A sales rep staying in a hotel in America went looking for the men's toilet. When at last he found it, it was already occupied. In desperation he went back to his room and relieved himself into a paper bag. When he had finished he was preparing to throw the bag out the window, which was on the first floor. Just as he had made his swing, the bottom of the bag gave way and he finished up with the contents all along the floor, up the wall, across the ceiling and down the opposite wall.

Aghast at the mess he had made, he offered $10 to a porter to clean up and say nothing about it. The porter just looked in amazement at the devastation and said:

"Man! I'll give you $20 if you'll just tell me what position you were in."

E ven if he is not required to use a "canned" sales story, every salesman who sells the same product over and over develops a patter of his own that is practically the same every time he takes a customer through it. The representatives of Grabbem & Shaggem were no exception. Indeed their range of products, and product types, was so great that a prepared story was the only way a salesman could cope. This had unexpected results when one salesman's mind wandered. He slipped a cog in his sales story and went off into the patter for an entirely different product.

They were doing a drive on Fluff wool shampoo with the grocers, while at the same time introducing Intimee vaginal deodorant pads to the chemists. With the latter it was often necessary to not only sell the friendly chemist, but also teach his girls how to sell the product to their customers.

The rep started by telling the girls about the desirability of using Intimee pads, which were entirely safe, and not only eliminated vaginal odour, but were perfumed with rose water as well. He then went on to explain that extensive research had produced a product that strengthened the natural fibres and through the action of ultraviolet light, gave them a colour that was better than the original. Matting and felting were reduced to a minimum and there was absolutely no shrinkage in the final product.

Everyone has seen the signs on cars in dealers' showrooms which advertise a basic price. On enquiry there are always a number of extras that have to be added on. Farmer Wilson had this experience when he bought his new car, so he was delighted when Honest Henry the dealer came to him to buy a cow.

Honest Henry inspected the herd closely and picked out a beast. Wilson told him:

"That there's a hundred dollar cow."

"Sounds okay," said Honest Henry reaching for his wallet. "I'll take her."

"Of course that's just the basic price," went on Wilson. "There are some extras." He did some calculations on a piece of paper and handed the result to his customer:

|  | $ |
|---|---|
| Basic cow | 100 |
| Two tone exterior | 35 |
| Additional stomach | 85 |
| Storage compartment & dispensing device | 70 |
| Four spigots @ $10 | 40 |
| Real cowhide upholstery | 65 |
| Dual horns @ $10 | 20 |
| Automatic fly swatter | 30 |
| TOTAL | $445 |

One rep had had a wall telephone at his home for years, and after much urging from his wife, finally arranged to have it replaced with a handset. The wall around the old telephone was covered with names and numbers, which were duly copied into a new telephone index. But six or eight numbers could not be identified. No one in the family claimed them. So one Saturday our man set to work to ring them all up, and find out who they were. One conversation stayed with him for a long time.

"Good afternoon. This is Arthur Greenway. I came across your telephone number without knowing whose it was. I just rang you up to find out, and to see if there is anything I can do for you."

"No thanks Arthur. You've done as much for me as I'd ever ask you to do. I'm your wife's first husband."

One Monday morning a customer walked into Riley's pharmacy with a complaint.

"Last Friday evening you sold me a gross of condoms, but when I opened them up there were only a hundred."

Riley was apologetic. He wrapped up forty-four condoms and passed them over to his customer.

"Hope we didn't spoil your weekend."

Making calls for the first time in a small town, a rep was making conversation with a storekeeper.

"What would the population of Millmerran be?"

"1,222."

"Is it growing very fast?"

"It isn't growing at all."

"But it must be, What was the population ten years ago?"

"1,222."

"That's the same as now. How come there isn't any growth?"

"Well, it's this way. Every time a girl in the town has a baby, some young fellow has to leave the district."

A produce salesman on his way to a farm is driving at nearly eighty kilometres per hour when out of nowhere comes a three-legged chicken that overtakes him and leaves him standing. The strange creature disappears over the hill. He is still shaken by the episode when he gets to the farm. He says to the farmer:

"The damnedest thing happened when I was on my way here. I'm doing nearly eighty and suddenly this three-legged chicken just shoots past. What's the story on this?"

"That's our three-legged chicken. We raised it."

"What did you want to raise a three-legged chicken for?"

"Well there's Mum and me and young Wilbur see? And whenever we had a chicken dinner we'd all want a drumstick. We used to kill two chickens, which was a waste, and there was a lot left over. So we started breeding three-legged chickens so each of us would get a drumstick."

"What do they taste like?"

"Dunno. We haven't been able to catch one yet."

There was an interview on television with North America's number one Salesman of the Year. The interviewer asked a number of the usual questions, where did you grow up, how did you get started in sales, and so on, then he said:

"You're the Salesman of the Year. Sell me something."

"What would you like me to sell you?"

There was an ashtray on the coffee table between them.

"How about that ashtray?"

"What do you want it for?"

"Well, it'll stop my friends from getting ash all over the carpet, and it'll fit in with the colour scheme of my living room, and besides that it's a nice looking ashtray."

"What do you think it might be worth?"

"Oh, about $8.50."

"It's yours."


A salesman once tried to sell a set of *Encyclopaedia Britannica* to an Irishman with a large family. He went through all the advantages of the encyclopaedia and pointed out that every one of his children would be able to take advantage of it.

The Irishman was not impressed.

"I'm thinkin' it'd be too dangerous. Why can't they walk to school the same as I did?"

One evening a rep got stuck in bumper-to-bumper traffic. His engine stopped and wouldn't start again. He got out and lifted the bonnet to see if he could find the trouble. While he was there he heard a strange noise, and walking round the car, found another driver squatting by his back wheel. This character grinned and winked and said:

"It's okay, mate. You get the battery and I'll get the hubcaps."

Retail sales reps are sometimes debt collectors too. One man knocked at the door of a girl's flat. When she opened the door he said:

"What about the next payment on that divan?"

The girl shrugged.

"Oh well. I suppose it's better than giving you money."

Federman, the knitwear king, got word that his top salesman had died from a heart attack while away on a country trip. He sent this telegram:

"RETURN SAMPLES BY GOODS RAIL AND SEARCH HIS POCKETS FOR ORDERS."

Corone's Hotel is very popular with sales reps because of its excellent cooking. It is a charming old world hotel, built around three sides of a square. It is more elaborately constructed than your average country hotel, but in the same general style of architecture.

Two of the boys, Claude and Cecil, booked into Corone's together late one afternoon. After dinner they went for a walk around the town, and arrived back at their hotel around eleven. No one had thought to tell them that the hotel was locked up at 10.30. After trying all the doors, the two walked round the back and into the open square courtyard. Claude pointed to the first floor verandah.

"There's our room. Up there. All we need now is a ladder."

A ladder was found and leant up against the verandah rail. The two began their ascent. Then Cecil said:

"Oh, Claude. I feel like a fireman."

"Don't be ridiculous, Cecil. Where are we going to get a fireman at this hour of the night?"

Finnegan returned to his old home town on a visit. While he was there he looked up his old friend Hennessy, who had the general store. He noticed as he went in that the two display windows were jammed full of soap. The two old friends greeted one another. As they did so, Finnegan saw that every shelf in the store was stacked with soap.

"Gosh! You've certainly got a lot of soap."

"You think so? Look at this."

He took Finnegan through to the storeroom which was also full of soap.

"I don't think I've ever seen so much soap."

"Come with me."

Hennessy lifted a trapdoor and took him down some steps into a huge cellar, which was jammed with soap from the floor to the roof.

"Gee! You really must sell a lot of soap."

"No, I don't actually. But the fellow that sold it to me — boy, could he sell soap!"

A young job applicant was being interviewed by the branch manager of a big wholesaler.

"If you join our organisation and work hard, who knows? One day you might become a representative or a buyer."

"Gosh!"

"Now a buyer is a man who knows more and more about less and less until finally he knows everything about nothing. Whereas a representative is a man who knows less and less about more and more until in the end he knows nothing about anything."

A salesman overnighting with a country family was to share a room with their seven-year-old boy. They undressed together and put on pyjamas but, before turning in, the lad knelt down beside the bed. The rep was impressed by this so he knelt down beside the boy. The boy was quite startled and said:

"What are you doing?"

"The same as you."

"Gosh! You won't half cop it from Mum. She hasn't put one down at that end."


A n American salesman was riding in the lower berth of a Pullman sleeping car. The woman in the upper berth leant over.

"I'm cold. Do you think you could get me another blanket?"

"Tell you what. Why don't we pretend we're married?"

"Well, all right."

"Okay. We're married. Get your own goddam blanket!"

A saleswoman travelling in French perfumes had car trouble late one Sunday afternoon. Fortunately she was not far from a farmhouse, so she walked over and interviewed the farmer.

"My car's broken down and I won't be able to get help until the morning. Can you put me up for the night?"

"Guess so, but I don't want any foolery with my two sons Dave and Bruce here." The two lads look to be in their early twenties.

"That'll be all right," she says.

But after they all go to bed, she starts to get randy just thinking about the two young men in the next room. In the end she sneaks in and wakes them.

"How would you boys like me to teach you the ways of the world?" The boys are willing.

"Only thing is, you'll have to wear these condoms in case I get pregnant." She helps them put them on and they go at it all night.

Four years go by and Dave takes Bruce aside.

"You remember that perfume saleslady that taught us the ways of the world?"

"Yeah," said Bruce, his eyes lighting up. "I remember."

"Do you care if she gets pregnant?"

"No."

"Neither do I. Let's take these damned things off."

A salesman was lying on the bed in his motel unit reading the Gideon Bible. He suddenly had an inspiration. Swinging to his feet he walked out of the unit and along the passage to reception. The girl on the desk was a pretty little redhead. He stopped and talked with her for a while.

"What time do you knock off?"

"Nine o'clock."

"What about coming round to my unit when you finish for a few drinks?"

"Well, I'd like to, but I don't know whether I should."

"It'll be okay. It says so in the Bible."

"Oh well, all right then. I'll see you at nine."

Soon after nine o'clock she showed up at his unit. He had some drinks ready.

"What about a brandy and dry?"

"It would be nice, but I don't know if I ought to."

"Course you can. It says so in the Bible."

"Well in that case, all right."

They had several drinks and then he suggested a little roll in the hay.

"I wish I could, but I don't know if it'd be okay."

"Of course it would. It says so in the Bible."

They both climbed into his bed and spent a very pleasant half hour or so. Then the girl asked:

"Anyway. Whereabouts in the Bible does it say that all this is okay?"

He reached for the Gideon Bible beside the bed, and opened the front cover where someone had written:

"The redhead on the reception desk is a sure thing."

Dave was down in the city. Business had been pretty good and he was shopping around for a new car. Dave didn't know very much about cars, but he was convinced that a good car should be well equipped with shock absorbers. He went into the Jaguar showroom and had a discussion with the salesman.

"It seems like a pretty good car, as you say, but how many shock absorbers has it got?"

"Two."

"Only two? The Mercedes has got four."

"Perhaps so, but there is really no comparison between the two."

"I'd like to buy your car, really I would. But I can't see myself buying a car that's only got two shock absorbers."

Seeing that he was about to lose a sale, the salesman tried another tack.

"Let me put it to you this way. How many tits has a cow got?"

"Four," said Dave.

"Right. And how many tits has Bo Derek got?"

"Two."

"Right. Now I ask you. Which gives you the better ride?"

On the afternoon of New Year's Eve, the licensee of the Prospector's Arms came into a wholesaler looking for some leis.

"I think we've got some," the salesman said. "I'll go down the back and check for you."

He looked in the store but there was not one left. He came back and broke the news to his customer.

"Sorry. We haven't got a single lei left."

"That's lovely. What am I supposed to do? You people sell decorations, and when I want to buy them you haven't got any."

He went on at length in this vein. The salesman waited his chance. When the customer stopped talking he said with a straight face:

"It's pretty tough when you can't get a lei on New Year's Eve, isn't it?"


A salesman of business machines became very enthusiastic about the capabilities of a new micro computer. This enthusiasm led him to claim to a public accountant that the machine would do half his work for him. It was a hot afternoon. The accountant fanned himself breathlessly. "All right," he said. "Give me two of them."

A sales rep working a new territory became hopelessly lost looking for a small town. He decided to ask for directions from a farmer. He stopped at the gate, got out of his car, opened the gate, got into his car and drove through. Then he stopped the car again, got out, closed the gate, and climbed back into his car again.

He drove up the long straight track to the yard outside the farmhouse, where the barking of the dogs soon brought the farmer out.

"What seems to be the trouble?"

"I'm trying to get through to Longfield and I've lost my way. Can you give me directions?"

"No. I don't think I can. I don't know the way myself."

The rep thanked the farmer anyway and turned his car around. He drove down the track to the gate and stopped his car. He got out, opened the gate, got in and drove through. He stopped the car again and got out. Just as he was closing the gate he heard a yell from the farmhouse. The farmer was beckoning him.

He opened the gate and went through the whole procedure again. Turn the car. Drive through the gate. Get out and shut the gate. Get in and drive back up to the farmhouse. The farmer was waiting for him.

"I thought I'd tell you. I asked the wife and she doesn't know the way to Longfield either."

Asking for directions in the Australian outback is often a chancy business. There was the rep who asked a farmer for directions to Goombungee.

"Take this road here for about two kilometres and turn left at the hollow log. You keep going for about three more kilometres and you'll come to Riley's dam. Turn left again. About four kilometres down the track you'll come to a big sign advertising sheep dip. Turn left there and keep going."

"And that'll get me to Goombungee, will it?"

"No. It'll get you back here. If I give you all the directions at once it'll only confuse you."


At the end of the school year Ken Jones took his ten-year-old son with him on a trip round his territory. The boy was thrilled to see for himself all the people and places he'd heard his dad talk about. After they came home there was all the ceremony of getting ready for Christmas.

On the great day the family were all surprised at the expensive presents Ken's youngster had bought for everyone. His mother asked him:

"Michael, where did you get the money for all these presents?"

"Easy, Mum. Everywhere Dad took me for a meal he left money on the table, so before we left I just picked it up."

A marketing consultant was brought in by a sales organisation in an effort to boost figures. The sales manager took him into his office and showed him a big wall map with red pins stuck in it.

"That's our sales area. All those red pins represent reps we've got in the field. The figures are just not good enough. I don't know what we're doing wrong."

"Well, the first thing you've got to do is take all the pins out of the map and stick them into your sales reps."


Max was travelling back to his territory by train. Sharing the compartment was an old farmer. The journey took them through some rich dairy country and the old fellow was giving Max a running commentary.

"That's Hanson's place there. That's a nice herd of cows he's got. Let's see. There's eighty-seven head there. This next farm is Sullivan's. He hasn't got a bad herd either. Let's see. There's sixty-five head there."

He went on in this vein until Max pulled him up.

"Hey, listen. You mean that you're actually counting these cows in the time it takes for the train to go past?"

"That's right."

"It's not possible."

"Oh, it's not so hard. There's a trick to it. I just count all the tits and divide by four."

Mancovits was a salesman. One day when he was driving across the Negev desert he came upon an Arab lying in the sand breathing his last. A compassionate man, he rushed to the poor man's side and took him in his arms. The Arab gasped:

"Water, effendi. Water."

"Are you in luck! Do you know that in my sample case I have the finest range of men's neckties this side of the King David Hotel. Normally $25 each—to you, only $21.50."

"Water, effendi. Water."

"You seem like a nice person. I'll tell you what. You can have any two ties in the range—polyester, silk, crepe—any two ties for only $35."

"Water, effendi. Water."

"You drive a hard bargain. Look. I'll let you have any tie you like—your pick—for $14.50. It's my rock bottom price."

"Water, effendi. Water."

"Oh! Water is it you want? Why didn't you say so. All you have to do is crawl to that sand dune over there, drop a right, and in five hundred metres you'll come to Poopie's Pyramid Club. He'll give you all the water you want."

With his last remaining strength the Arab dragged himself to the sand dune, turned right and crawled on his elbows to the club.

Poopie was standing in the doorway. The Arab gasped:

"Water, effendi. Water."

"Ah, water is it you want eh? I got all kinds of water—ice water, soda water, mineral water, seltzer water—all kinds of water, on the inside. Only thing is, you can't come in without a tie."

A sales rep came home to his apartment unexpectedly in the middle of the day. As he let himself in he heard giggling and scuffling. Once inside he demanded of his wife:

"Who have you got here in the apartment with you?"

"Nobody. I'm on my own."

"I don't believe you. I'll look for myself."

He searched the apartment without finding anyone and then happened to look over the balcony. They were on the fifth floor. Below him he saw a man climbing from the fourth to the third floor.

"There he is, the bastard."

In a fit of rage he grabbed the refrigerator and threw it over the balcony onto the figure below, who was killed at once.

In a fit of jealousy his wife promptly stabbed him to death with a carving knife.

Presently, there appeared at the Pearly Gates three men. St Peter asked the first:

"What's your story?"

The jealous husband related the events leading up to his death.

"I see," said St Peter. "And what about you?"

"I was cleaning the windows of this apartment building. As I was climbing from the fourth floor down to the third, I was hit by a refrigerator."

"Sorry about that," said the salesman.

St Peter turned to the third man.

"And what brings you here?"

"I'm really not sure. There I was just sitting inside this refrigerator . . ."

A salesman was making an overnight journey in the slowest, most miserable train he had ever seen. He had reserved a sleeping berth, but was not at all encouraged when he inspected it. There was a tiny compartment off the corridor, with few amenities, and the two berths were one above the other.

When the train moved off, there was no sign of any traveller to occupy the other berth, so, when he was ready to turn in, he settled himself in the upper berth to avoid having someone climb past him during the night.

He slept fitfully. Whenever the train stopped he would be awakened by the lights and shouting on the platform. Only when they moved off would he doze off until the next station.

It was after one such stop, at about midnight, that the rep was abruptly awakened by a loud bang as the sliding door of his compartment was flung open. This was followed by two heavy thumps as two suitcases were hurled in.

The salesman was ready to express his opinion of this lack of consideration when he saw from his vantage point that his travelling companion was a good-looking blonde.

He moved back almost out of sight and, with one eye peering over the edge of the bunk, he watched the young woman first unpack a few things, and then proceed to disrobe.

When she had divested herself of nearly all her garments, and the salesman was beginning to really enjoy the show, he was rather taken aback to see her remove a blonde wig and toss it on the shelf. She was as bald as an egg.

Next came a full set of false teeth which she soaked in a glass. Then she took out a glass eye which was carefully placed in a velvet-lined box.

By the time she had removed a pair of false breasts, and unhitched an artificial leg, the rep was flabbergasted.

At this point she caught sight of him, his eyes bugging over the top bunk.

"What the bloody hell do you want?" she demanded.

"You know what I want. Unscrew it and hand it up."

A rep looking for accommodation in a country town found a place offering a room and full board for only $25 a week. He moved right in. His first meal was breakfast—stewed rabbit. He hadn't eaten rabbit for a good while so he didn't mind at all. For lunch they had fried rabbit. At dinner it was roast rabbit. This went on day after day.

On the fourth morning the rep didn't show up for breakfast, so the landlady went to his room. He was doubled up, holding his stomach and groaning. She said:

"You poor man. You're not well. I'll call the doctor."

"Never mind the doctor," was the reply. "Get me a ferret."

A man won a major prize in a lottery and invested his winnings in a plastics factory making toothbrushes. For several months they kept making toothbrushes and stock-piling them in a warehouse.

When his money was beginning to run low he realised that he needed to sell his toothbrushes, so he advertised for a sales representative. The only applicant was a scruffy individual who had been working on a garbage truck, but who badly wanted a chance to break into sales. Since he was the only applicant, the employer decided to give him a chance.

"I'll give you $50 petty cash to start you off."

"What's petty cash?"

"That's in case you have to buy anything, or buy a drink for someone."

"Can you give me any clues how to go about it? It's all new to me."

"Well, you want to go where there are plenty of people. And it'll help if you can think up some kind of gimmick."

At the end of his first week the new rep came in to report.

"How many toothbrushes did you sell?"

"Seven thousand, six hundred and sixty-two."

"That's very good. How did you go about it?"

"I did what you said and went where there were plenty of people. I went to the biggest railway station in town. I used the $50 you gave me to buy a card table and a couple of big basins. I set up the card table with one basin full of potato crisps, and the other one full of dip. Then I kept yelling out, 'Free dip! Free dip!' Then a guy would come up and grab a crisp, dip it in the dip, and stuff it in his mouth. Then he'd choke and say, 'This tastes like shit.' I'd say, 'It is. Wanna buy a toothbrush?'"

A rep driving through the country became completely lost, but finally came to a small town. He stopped at a house to ask directions.

"What's the name of this place?" he asked the man who came to the door.

"Queersville."

"That's a funny name. Why do they call it that?"

"I don't know. I'll ask my wife. Hey, Wilbur . . ."

An American salesman was travelling in folding ironing boards. He had an upper berth in the Pullman car. He struck up a conversation with a woman in the upper berth across the aisle. Pretty soon he was inviting her to come over and visit with him for a while. She was reluctant.

"How am I going to get over there?"

"Easy. I've got something good and solid here that I can put across the aisle between the berths. You can cross over on that."

"Well, I suppose it'll be all right."

From one of the lower berths came the voice of an old lady:

"Don't you do it, dearie. How do you think he's going to get you back?"

Confucius say: representative who cover chair instead of territory always stay on bottom.

A salesman stopped at a farm and asked the farmer if he could use the toilet. The farmer said:

"Sure you can, son, but it's a bit of a mess. Y'see, my wife takes salts."

The rep made his way up the back path to the outhouse, where he was shocked to see that the farmer had not been exaggerating—the walls, the floor, and the ceiling were all covered with shit. Somehow he used it and made his escape outside as soon as he could.

He thanked the farmer and asked him:

"What kind of salts does your wife take?"

"Somersaults."


L ester went off on a country trip, but had gone only three blocks before he realised that he had left his call cards on the coffee table. He went back home and quietly went into the house. His wife was at the sink in a filmy negligee. She was so inviting that he sneaked up behind her and put his hand on her breast. Without turning round she said:

"Just one litre will do today, thanks. Lester's away on a trip for the rest of the week."

It was hot and dry and dusty. To make matters ten times worse there was a beer shortage. A rep walked into a bar and ordered a beer.

"Are you an RC?"

"What difference does religion make? All I want is a beer."

"What I meant was, are you a regular customer?"

The rep admitted that he wasn't and walked down the street to another pub. Once in the bar he said to the girl:

"I'm an RC, and I want a couple of beers."

"I don't care about your religion, but where are your glasses?"

"I don't wear them."

The girl was exasperated.

"Beer glasses, mate. Ours were all busted last night in a brawl."

There was one pub left in the town. When he walked into the bar he spotted two glasses on the window sill. He grabbed them and took them to the bar. The barmaid looked at them.

"What are you trying to do? You've had your quota."

A salesman walked into the parlour of a country pub and was amazed to see a poker game in progress where one of the players was a sheepdog. As he watched, the dog drew two cards and took out the jackpot with a full hand.

"This is unreal," said the salesman. "I've never seen anything like it. There can't be another dog in the country that can play cards like this one."

"Ah, he's not that hard to beat. Every time he gets a good hand he wags his tail."

The entire North American sales force of Frisky Dog Food was gathered together for their national sales convention at Miami Beach. In the great auditorium the marketing director was giving a performance that any revivalist would have been proud of. Using the old pattern of call and response, he was really working up the spirits of his sales team.

"Who's got the greatest dog food in North America?"
"We have!"
"And who's got the greatest advertising campaigns?"
"We have!"
"Who's got the most attractive packages?"
"We have!"
"Who's got the biggest distribution?"
"WE HAVE!"
"Okay. So why aren't we selling more of the product?"
One bold voice from the crowd replied:
"Because the damned dogs don't like it."

Two sales managers were talking at a trade exhibition.
One asked the other:

"How do you get hold of such terrific salespeople?"

"I use special testing techniques. One of them is to send
a man out looking for a flat while carrying a trombone."

There was a young lad named Terry working the petrol
pumps at Eastgate Motors where most of the reps got
their petrol. He was really keen on cars. He studied every
different make and model that came in for petrol. He was
really thrilled one afternoon when a customer drove in
in a Cadillac. It was the first he had seen. After he'd filled
it up he quizzed the owner about all the gadgets.

"What's that long black thing on the dashboard?"

"That's an automatic sensor that detects the headlights
of an oncoming car, and dips the lights for you."

"And what about those controls over there?"

"That's the cruise control. You can set that for any speed
and it keeps the car going at just that speed automatically."

Next it was the radar detector. Then Terry noticed a
couple of golf tees lying on the top of the dashboard.

"What are those things for?"

"Those are what I rest my balls on when I drive."

"Gosh!" said Terry. "The Cadillac people really think
of everything don't they?"

The phone rang in the real estate agency. The woman on the line enquired:

"Do you sell maternity fashions?"

The salesman thought fast.

"No, madam, we don't. But perhaps we can interest you in a larger house."

The star salesman of the life insurance company was the agent who worked the rural communities. Wherever he went he took along with him an all-round hired hand. Whatever the farmer was doing when they arrived, the hired hand offered to do it for him. Glad of the break, the farmer was then free to listen to the salesman's story.

That real estate salesman is too good for me. He sold me a piece of land that turned out to be under water. When I went back to see him about it, he sold me a motor boat.

The Avon lady has added a new dimension to salesmanship. One has a line for housewives that always brings results:

"Here's something that your neighbours said you couldn't afford."

Another Avon lady has a great door-opener:
"You'll never guess what I just saw in your neighbour's bedroom. May I come in and tell you about it?"

The street vendor was very persuasive.
"Take home a bunch of flowers for the wife, sir."
"I don't have a wife."
"Then take a bunch for your sweetheart."
"I haven't got a sweetheart either."
"You're a lucky man. Buy a couple of bunches to celebrate."

A young man shyly crept into the office of the sales manager.
"You don't want to buy any insurance do you?"
"No I don't."
"I thought as much." He turned to go.
"Wait a minute. I've been working with salespeople all my life and I've never seen such a poor approach as yours. You'll never make any sales because you lack confidence. Tell you what I'll do. I'll give you confidence by proving you can make a sale. You can write me up for $100 000."
When the proposal had been completed, the sales manager said:
"Now that you have confidence, you should learn some of the tricks of the trade."
"Thank you very much. You're quite right about the tricks of the trade, of course. The one I just used is for sales managers."

The salesman was staying at a farmhouse, and sleeping in the same bed as the farmer's daughter. He made a pass at her but she said:

"Stop that or I'll call my father."

A little later he made another try and got the same response:

"Stop that or I'll call my father."

She did move closer though, and on his third try he was successful. A little while later she said to him:

"Could we do it again?"

He agreed of course. Later as he was dozing off she said:

"Can we do it again?"

He again rose to the occasion. But five minutes later she was tugging at this sleeve.

"Can we do it again?"

"Stop that or I'll call your father."


The country storekeeper was out of stock of a popular item. Asked if he'd have it in stock soon he replied:

"No I won't."

"Why not?"

"Moves too fast."

One salesman has a line he uses on the phone that he says gets him through to a busy executive every time. When the receptionist asks:

"What was it in connection with?"

He always answers:

"I want to know what he's going to do about my daughter."

The Taxation Department queried a claim from a bachelor salesman for a dependant daughter. The note said:

"This must have been a typist's error."

He sent the report back with a note that said:

"It certainly was."

The sales manager's job was getting him down. After dinner he just slumped into an armchair with a stiff drink. His wife climbed into his lap to chat him up about a new fur coat. She cuddled him and caressed him and fondled him until at last he snapped:

"For heaven's sake, Margaret, get off. Don't you think I get enough of that at work?"

Two reps were talking about their sex lives.

"Do you know, I never had any relations with my wife until we were married. Did you?"

"I don't know. What was your wife's maiden name?"

Two salesman were writing up their orders in the reps' room. One asked the other:

"How did the big date go last night?"

"Terrible. The minute we got back to her flat the phone started ringing with fellows trying to get a date. It never stopped."

"Well, an attractive young woman's got to have her number in the phone book hasn't she?"

"Maybe so, but not in the Yellow Pages."

A Jewish agent worked with an insurance broker whose directors were all good Catholics. He did exceptionally well and they all agreed that he should be made a director. The agent's religion did present a problem, however, as the board did not believe it wise to have a non-Catholic as a partner. In the end they called in a Catholic priest to convert the Jewish insurance agent. The two men were alone in an office for more than two hours. Finally they came out. The managing director asked the priest:

"Did you succeed in converting our Jewish agent?"

"No I didn't, but he did sell me $100 000 worth of life insurance."

After the summer vacation Mike came back to work tanned and rested. One of the other reps asked him about his time off.

"Well, a friend of mine asked me up to his place in the country — quiet, secluded, no night life, no parties, and no women within a hundred kilometres."

"Did you enjoy yourself?"

"Who went?"


One of the reps took out a girl from the typing pool. She was lovely to look at but didn't have many brains. At the end of the night he took her home to his apartment. She looked vacantly at all his books and paintings. Then she pointed to a carved wooden ornament over the fireplace.

"Whatever's that?"

"It's African. They use it in fertility rites. It's actually a phallic symbol."

"Really? I'd hate to tell you what it looks like."


Two sales reps were having coffee.

"How's business?"

"You know how it is. Our line's like sex. When it's good it's wonderful; when it's bad it's still okay. How are you getting on?"

"Couldn't be worse. Even the customers who don't pay their bills have stopped buying."

A sales rep in Miami turned in where he saw a big neon sign: "Motel—TV." When he got to his unit and unpacked he was annoyed to find that there was no television set in the suite. He rang the manager:

"How can I watch television without a television set?"

"Who said anything about a television set?"

"What about that sign outside—TV?"

"Oh, that. That stands for tourists velcome."

Max was belting along the highway at high speed when he hit a patch of loose gravel and went over an embankment. Another driver stopped to help him. As he pulled Max out of his car he asked:

"Have you been drinking?"

"What a stupid question. Of course I've been drinking. Do you think I drive like this sober?"

A used car salesman tells us that the little old lady who only used the car on Sundays has been replaced by a nymphomaniac who only used the back seat.

A salesman visiting a farm was amazed to see a pig walking round the yard with a wooden leg. He asked the farmer about it.

"That pig is really the most wonderful pig that ever was. One time I fell asleep in the barn and while I was asleep the barn caught fire. Do you know that pig actually broke out of his pen and came into the flames to drag me to safety. I owe my life to that pig."

"That's certainly very impressive, but you haven't told me why it's got a wooden leg."

"Well, a wonderful pig like that—you can't just eat it all at once."


A door-to-door salesman asked a small boy: "Is your mother at home?"

"Yes, she is."

But after knocking for quite a while and getting no answer, he asked the boy again:

"I thought you said your mother was at home."

"She is, but we don't live here."


*Buyer*: I can't see you today. You'll have to arrange an appointment with my secretary.

*Salesman*: I tried that but she's booked up for the next two weeks.

When Rupert was shown in to see his customer, Mr Jones was staring out the window disconsolately.

"What seems to be the trouble?"

"I promised my wife a Pomeranian and the cheapest one I can get is $200. It's too much."

"You're right. I can sell you one for $125."

"Great! When can you deliver it?"

"I'll let you know."

Once outside he rushed to a public telephone and rang his sales manager.

"Listen. I've just sold old Jonesy a Pomeranian for $125. What the hell is a Pomeranian?"


Two reps met in a cafe. One asked:

"Why are you eating only dry biscuits and cheese? Are you on a diet?"

"No. I'm on commission."


A salesman for the local paper called on Riley the chemist.

"No way. I've been in business forty-one years and never spent a penny on advertising yet."

"Really? Then you can tell me, what is that handsome building on the top of the hill?"

"That's St Catherine's church."

"Been there long?"

"Over a hundred years."

"They still ring the bell, don't they?"

Customer: "Are those eggs fresh?"

Grocer: "Feel the eggs, Henry. See if they're cool enough to sell."

Customer: "I've come back to buy that car you showed me yesterday."

Salesman: "Great. I thought you might. What was the main factor that made you decide to buy?"

Customer: "My wife."

A sales rep was stuck in a small northern town during a cyclone. There was one pool room, but all the balls were dirty grey.

"How can you tell which is which?"

"If you play here long enough, you learn to tell them by the shape."

One energetic salesman wanting to see a buyer finally got past all the secretaries at the end of the day. His prospect said:

"You're a salesman, eh? Do you know my girls have thrown out fifteen salesmen today already?"

"Yes sir. I'm them."

A book salesman was offering to farmers a volume titled *How To Farm Better and Make More Money.* He wasn't having much luck at all. Finally he asked one farmer:

"Why don't you buy this book? Don't you want to farm better and make more money?"

The farmer shook his head sadly.

"Son, I ain't farming half as well as I know how to *now.*"

A salesman was arrested for selling youth pills. He promised his customers eternal youth. When the police charged him at the station they checked his record. He had been arrested on the same charges in 1791, 1862 and 1901.

Salesmanship has been defined as the difference between seduction and rape.

Driving down a back road, a salesman had trouble with his car. He stopped and lifted the bonnet to see if he could find the trouble. A voice behind him said:

"The trouble is in the battery."

When he looked around there was no one there except an old sway-backed horse. He was so rattled by this that he jumped into the car and took off. Twenty minutes later he came to a town with a small service station. He told his story to the owner.

"There was no one there except you and the horse?"

"Right."

"Was it a black, sway-backed horse with bow legs?"

"That's the one."

"Don't take any notice of him. He doesn't know a thing about engine trouble."

Two women were talking in the supermarket.

"Harry's away so much on business trips now that when he does come home he's like a total stranger."

"How thrilling!"

Then there was the sales manager who opened up the sales meeting by announcing:

"Ladies and gentlemen, the purpose of this meeting is to fire you with enthusiasm. If it doesn't work I'm going to fire you—with enthusiasm."

A housewife who was hard of hearing answered the door to find a salesman with a large sample case.

"Good morning, madam. I'm representing the Wonderwarm Woollen Works. We're offering discount prices on yarns that didn't come up to our proper standards. The colours ran and the yarns are a bit off-colour. Could I come in and show you my samples?"

"I'm sorry. I'm hard of hearing. What did you say?"

The salesman raised his voice.

"Would you be interested in some off-colour yarns?"

"Sounds like fun. Come in for a cup of coffee and you can tell them to me."

The sales manager was taking a rep to task about his reports.

"They're awful. Nobody can make head or tail of them. A good report should be written so that any fool can understand it easily."

"I couldn't agree more. Which part of the report can't you understand?"

A minister bought a used car which "had belonged to a little old lady school teacher". A few days later he drove back to the dealer and told the salesman:

"I came to return some things your little old lady left in the glove box—a bottle of scotch and a carton of cigarettes."

A really tough-looking customer goes to the fruit and vegetable section of a supermarket and asks to buy half a lettuce.

"You can't buy half a lettuce. We only sell them whole."

"Is that right?" The customer tears a lettuce in half and takes it to the check-out. The cashier tells him he'll have to check the price with the manager. He walks over to the manager and says:

"There's a dumb-looking ape out here wants to buy just half a lettuce." Then he glances back and sees that his customer has followed him, and has heard every word. He quickly goes on, ". . . and this friendly customer has offered to buy the other half."

Several days later the manager tells the cashier:

"I like a man who can think on his feet. I believe you'd make a good store manager. I'm arranging for you to attend a training course in Winnipeg, Canada."

"Winnipeg? The only people who come from Winnipeg are either whores or hockey players."

"Is that so? You might be interested to know that my wife comes from Winnipeg."

"Really? What position did she play?"